Bible Memory Games

Ages Six through Twelve

NEXGEN

Building the New Generation of Believers

An Imprint of Cook Communications Ministries
COLORADO SPRINGS, COLORADO • PARIS, ONTARIO
KINGSWAY COMMUNICATIONS, LTD., EASTBOURNE, ENGLAND

NexGen® is an imprint of
Cook Communications Ministries, Colorado Springs, CO 80918
Cook Communications, Paris, Ontario
Kingsway Communications, Eastbourne, England

BIBLE MEMORY GAMES
© 2004 by Cook Communications Ministries

First Printing, 2004
Printed in the United States of America
1 2 3 4 5 6 7 8 9 10 Printing/Year 08 07 06 05 04

Editorial Manager: Doug Schmidt
Product Developer: Karen Pickering
Design: Granite Design
Illustrations: Heiser Graphics

ISBN 0-7814-4119-6

Table of Contents

Ball, Balloon, and Beanbag Games

Chalkboard or Whiteboard Games

Games That Don't Need Supplies

Games with a Variety of Supplies

Games with Puppets

Music and Rhythm Games

Paper Games

Puzzle Games

Introduction

What a privilege to help children memorize God's Word! However, we know that oftentimes our methods become rote and the desire to learn is diminished. *Bible Memory Games* is intended to provide you—the teacher—with alternative games and activities to help children memorize Bible verses without getting bored. We hope that you will find these games and activities fun and entertaining, yet help children more easily learn the Bible memory verses you are studying.

As you will see when you begin reading each specific game or activity, there are no specific Bible verses given to you. Because we have not written each game or activity to reflect a particular Bible verse, you have the flexibility to incorporate this into your current curriculum. You have the freedom to teach an entire verse or even part of a verse. In addition, these games can be a great break in your lesson to get kids moving around during classroom time.

Be sure to look over your situation carefully as you plan to use these games and activities. For example, do you have a room that is large enough to accommodate a group of children playing a game with balls or balloons? Or, is your room smaller, so you'll need to focus on games and activities that keep children close to their chairs? Whatever your situation, you can find appropriate games and activities to reinforce what you are already teaching in your lesson. You can also make plans to take the children outside for some of these games and activities if the weather is nice.

Another item to keep in mind is the age of the children in your class. If you are teaching young elementary children, then you will want to concentrate on games and activities that are age appropriate for children in kindergarten through second grade. Be sure to keep in mind the reading level of your students.

If you are working with beginning readers, plan your games and activities accordingly. If an activity suggests writing words onto shapes, the whiteboard, or a poster, consider one of the following suggestions.

• You may find that you can replace some of the words with pictures to help the children "read" the verse. Look for words that suggest pictures. For example, if your verse says, "I am the light of the world," then find some simple pictures of a light and the earth. Replace those words with the pictures.

• When working with the Bible memory verse, always read the verse aloud with your class two or three times. This helps the children hear the words and begin to associate them with the written words.

• Always be prepared to help any child decode a word that is difficult for them. Don't make an issue of this fact, just say the words if they are struggling and help them to the conclusion.

Be sure to also be aware of potential reading difficulties for older elementary children. If you notice a child that appears to be struggling with an activity, quietly move in to help him or her. If you are using team games, try grouping your students so that you have a mixture of both stronger and weaker readers. Older elementary children sometimes stay on the periphery if they are having difficulty. Be there to help them and encourage them (without embarrassing them) to try to participate in the game or activity.

We have also provided several pages with patterns to help you prepare some of the games and activities. This may take a bit of advance preparation but it is well worth the effort. If you choose to photocopy and enlarge the animals (or other items), you might consider making them on poster board. When you have the animal drawn and cut out, cover the whole piece with clear, self-adhesive paper. You can then write on the piece with a crayon or erasable marker. When finished with that particular Bible memory activity, you can wipe the piece clean and store it to use for the same game or a similar one at a different time.

Be sure to read over the supply list that follows this section. If you have your supplies gathered in advance, then it is easy to pull together any game or activity at a moment's notice. Some of the standard supplies may be available in your church or classroom. For other supplies, you can ask parents to help provide them at the beginning of the year or teaching cycle. If parents know the reason for the request, they are usually very eager to help provide the needed supplies.

There are times when you might want to have a helper in your classroom to assist you. The youth in your church might be willing to be assistants on a rotating basis. It is always helpful to have another individual when you play some of the team games or if you have a very large class. Don't hesitate to ask for assistance. It may be worthwhile to plan a "helper party" to explain what the helper needs to do when they are in your classroom. You could ask them to come for a special half-hour session and provide cookies and soda. Show them where the supplies are kept so they can assist you. If you have time, you could play one or two of the games with them to help them understand what you will be doing in your classroom when they assist you. If youth are not available, you can ask parents to help on an as-needed basis.

As you teach Bible memory verses, you can be sure the children will gain a lasting appreciation of those particular verses. Many of the children will remember those verses for the rest of their lives. And remember—have fun with the children!

Supply List

FURNITURE
- ❑ Chairs
- ❑ Chalkboard or whiteboard
- ❑ Chalk or whiteboard markers
- ❑ Eraser

MISCELLANEOUS
- ❑ Felt in dark brown
- ❑ Felt in a light color
- ❑ Felt board
- ❑ String or yarn
- ❑ Balls of yarn
- ❑ Dried lima beans
- ❑ Colorful O-shaped cereal
- ❑ Balloons
- ❑ Beanbags
- ❑ Soft balls
- ❑ Net bag (such as for produce or laundry)
- ❑ Baby doll
- ❑ Basket or box for doll
- ❑ Cell phone or child's play phone
- ❑ Three or more cuddly stuffed animals
- ❑ Small toys or objects that relate to words in your Bible verses
- ❑ Real or toy pennies
- ❑ Decorative pillowcases

MUSICAL SUPPLIES
- ❑ Music CDs
- ❑ CD player
- ❑ Cassette recorder
- ❑ Blank cassette tapes
- ❑ CD player or karaoke machine with microphone
- ❑ Rhythm instruments

PAPER SUPPLIES
- ❑ Butcher paper
- ❑ Clear, self-adhesive paper
- ❑ Construction paper
- ❑ Copy paper
- ❑ Drawing paper
- ❑ Index cards
- ❑ Newspaper
- ❑ Newsprint paper
- ❑ Poster board
- ❑ Scrap paper
- ❑ Brown paper grocery bags

PATTERNS
- ❑ Stepping-stone (pattern included in book)
- ❑ Paper crown (pattern included in book)
- ❑ Animal outlines (patterns included in book)
- ❑ Access to photocopy machine

PUPPETS
- ❑ Hand puppets
- ❑ Bird puppet or toy bird

SCHOOL SUPPLIES
- ❑ Scissors for children and adults
- ❑ Glue
- ❑ Pencils and pens
- ❑ Markers, washable
- ❑ Markers, permanent
- ❑ Sidewalk chalk
- ❑ Watercolor paints
- ❑ Paintbrush
- ❑ Masking tape
- ❑ Disposable wipes

Notes

Action Games

1. Action Verse

Supplies: None

Preparation: Choose a Bible verse that supports the lesson. Try to choose a verse that lends itself to actions. Then think of full-body actions that represent key words or phrases of the verse, such as kneeling, reaching up high, patting another on the back, and so on.

First, silently do the full-body actions for the children and see if they can guess what concepts you are motioning. As the children guess, tell them the specific words or phrases related to those actions. Then have the children imitate your actions while saying those words.

After showing all the actions, say the verse from the beginning, putting the actions in where they belong. Act out the verse several times, encouraging the children to join you on the actions and words as they learn them. Once the verse is learned, divide the class in half to face each other. Have one half of the class say the verse while the other half does the actions. Have the groups switch roles.

2. Arm Link Game

Supplies: None

Preparation: Choose a Bible verse to learn or review.

Practice the Bible verse a few times to familiarize the children with it. Then have the children stand around the room. The children will "get along" by linking arms and saying the verse together. First, the children walk at random around the room, saying the verse. At your signal, each child links arms with another child, and the pairs say the verse. Give another signal. Each pair links arms with another pair, and these new groups repeat the verse. Continue playing the game until all the children in the room are linked.

3. Bible Trail

Supplies: Poster board, scissors, marker, masking tape, (optional: clear, self-adhesive paper)

Preparation: Choose a Bible verse to learn or review. Cut the poster board into large squares. Make enough squares to equal the number of words in the memory verse, including the reference. Print each word of the verse on a separate square in large letters. You may want to cover the squares with clear, self-adhesive paper. If you have a large group, make two or three sets of cards. Tape each Bible verse square, in order, onto the floor in a trail pattern. Be creative about where the trail goes. (Tape firmly so the squares don't slip out from under the children and cause a fall.)

Say the verse together with the class a few times. Then let the children take turns walking down the Bible Trail, saying the word on each card. The rest of the class may recite or clap as a child walks.

4. Circles of Friends

Supplies: None

Preparation: Choose a Bible verse that supports the lesson or that reviews a verse the children have previously learned.

Have the children stand in two circles, a smaller circle inside a larger one. The circles of children will walk in opposite directions (one clockwise and one counterclockwise.) The children will repeat the verse as they walk in their circles. As they walk past each other, they will give the child in the other circle a high five (raising one hand and gently slapping the other person's raised hand). After repeating the verse a few times, the circles can change directions and the verse can be repeated again.

5. Building the Temple

Supplies: None

Preparation: Choose a Bible verse to learn or review.

Tell the children that they will help "build the temple" by saying the memory verse. Have the children hold hands and form a circle. Say the memory verse together.

Next help the circle step forward to turn the circle into the four "sides" of a square or rectangle (still holding hands). Say the memory verse again. Have the children on one side hold their hands up to make arches for the temple. Have the class repeat the verse. Then the children on a second side hold their hands up. Repeat the verse again. Do the same for the third and fourth sides. If you would like the children to have more practice, you could let each "stone" of the temple (each child) say the verse alone.

6. Creative Groups

Supplies: None

Preparation: Choose a memory verse that supports lesson or one that reinforces a verse the children have been learning in Sunday school.

Say the verse phrase by phrase, and have the class echo each phrase after you. Say the verse in this manner a few times. Be sure the kids understand what all the words mean.

Divide the children into small groups. Each group has the task of making up hand motions to represent words or phrases in the verse. Encourage originality, but some groups may end up with similar motions. You might want to print the verse on the board for the kids to refer to.

When done, have the groups take turns saying and showing the verse to the others.

7. Duck, Duck, Verse

Supplies: None

Preparation: Choose a Bible verse to learn or review.

This memory game is similar to "Duck, Duck, Goose." Have the children sit in a circle. Say the verse together several times. Then choose one child to walk around the outside of the circle and tap each seated child on the head. Rather than saying "duck" or "goose," the tapper says the memory verse, one word on each tap. On the reference, the child tapped jumps up and chases the tapper around the circle. Whoever reaches the open seat in the circle first sits down, and the other child becomes the new tapper.

8. Follow the Leader

Supplies: None
Preparation: Choose a memory verse that supports or reinforces a verse learned in Sunday school.

Say the verse a line at a time, and have the class repeat it after you. Do this a few times until the verse is familiar.

Then let volunteers take turns "leading" the class in a different way to say the verse. They might instruct the class to say it with both hands on their head, while standing on one foot, or by whispering it. Emphasize that the leaders need to make good choices as they lead.

9. Growing a Verse

Supplies: None
Preparation: Choose a Bible verse for the children to memorize or review.

Explain that the children will "grow" as they practice saying the verse. Have everyone crouch down. Say a phrase from the verse, and have the class repeat it as they raise up a tiny bit. Say the next phrase and have the class raise up a little higher. Repeat until the whole verse has been said and the children are reaching up high. Repeat the activity a few more times until the verse is familiar to the children.

10. Hidden Verse

Supplies: Construction paper, scissors
Preparation: Choose a Bible verse for the children to memorize or review. From construction paper, cut a small heart shape for each word in the verse and the reference. Write each word on a heart. Write the reference on a separate heart. Hide the hearts around the room.

Say the memory verse with the children. Then tell them to find the hearts hidden around the room with those words on them. Make sure every child finds a heart. As the children search, repeat the verse together. When all the hearts are found, have the kids put the verse in order on the floor. As a group, say the verse together several times.

11. Hopscotch

Supplies: Index cards or poster board, marker, masking tape (optional: clear, self-adhesive paper)

Preparation: Choose a Bible verse to learn or review. Write each word of the memory verse on a separate index card or square of poster board. You may want to cover the squares or cards with clear, self-adhesive paper. With masking tape, mark off a large hopscotch pattern on the floor. Securely tape each word of the verse to a square in order. The hopscotch board may be longer or shorter than usual, depending on the length of the verse.

Read the verse to the children, and talk about what it means. Have a volunteer demonstrate how to hop on the hopscotch pattern and read each word of the verse as it is hopped on.

Have the children line up behind the hopscotch pattern. Let the first child say the verse while hopping on the squares. Have the children wait until the person ahead of them has finished before they begin.

Let children who think they know the verse try hopping and saying the words by memory rather than by reading the words on the squares. Help younger children who can't read by saying the verse with them.

12. Hop the Verse

Supplies: Poster board or cardboard, marker, masking tape
Preparation: Choose a memory verse that supports the
lesson. The verse could be a verse learned earlier. Clearly print
each word of the verse and the reference on a square of
cardboard or poster board. If you have a large group, make two
or three sets.

Introduce the memory verse by saying it aloud, phrase by
phrase, and having the class repeat after you. Do this a few
times until the verse is familiar to the children.

Lay the verse squares on the floor in a winding path, but
slightly mix up the words so that the children have to think
about the order they are walking in. Tape the squares in
place. The children will hop or walk to each word in the
correct order, saying the words aloud as they go. (You might
prefer that the kids step next to the square rather on them
to avoid slipping or tearing.)

If your class is large, divide the kids into two or three
groups, each with its own verse path. You could make the
paths fun and challenging by having them intersect.

13. Jumpin' Squares

Supplies: Chairs
Preparation: Choose a Bible verse for the children to
memorize. Set up the chairs in the shape of a square with the
seats facing inward.

Divide the children into four groups and have each group
sit on one side of the square. Say the Bible memory verse
together a few times, with the kids repeating each phrase
after you to help them start to learn it.

Explain to the children that they will take turns saying
the words of the verse. Group 1 jumps up, says the first
word, and sits down. Group 2 jumps up, says the second
word, and sits down. Continue going around the square
until the whole verse has been said. Next have the groups
say the verse phrase by phrase. For added practice, mix up
the groups. For example, have groups 1 and 3 jump up to
say a word or phrase. Before finishing, have the groups take
turns standing to say the whole verse.

14. Meaningful Motions

Supplies: None

Preparation: Choose a memory verse to learn or review. Think of simple whole-body actions that represent key words or phrases of the verse.

Say the verse slowly while doing the whole-body actions for the children. Repeat it a few times, and encourage the children to join you on the actions. As the verse becomes familiar, have the children join you in saying it along with doing the actions.

Divide the children into pairs and have them stand facing each other. Have the pairs say the verse together while watching each other do the actions. Then have the children turn around and find a different child to pair with and say the verse again. Have the children keep forming different pairs to give them practice saying the verse.

15. Pop-up Practice

Supplies: None

Preparation: Choose a Bible verse for the children to review or memorize. Print the verse on the board.

If most of your class can read, let volunteers take turns leading the class in saying it. If you have nonreaders, assign children who can read to be their partners.

Seat everyone in a circle. Choose a child to start by jumping up and saying the first word, then sitting down quickly. The next child pops up to the say the next word, then sits down. Continue in this way around the circle. Go around the circle again, this time with each "popper" saying two or three words at a time. Challenge the kids to do it as quickly as possible with no mistakes.

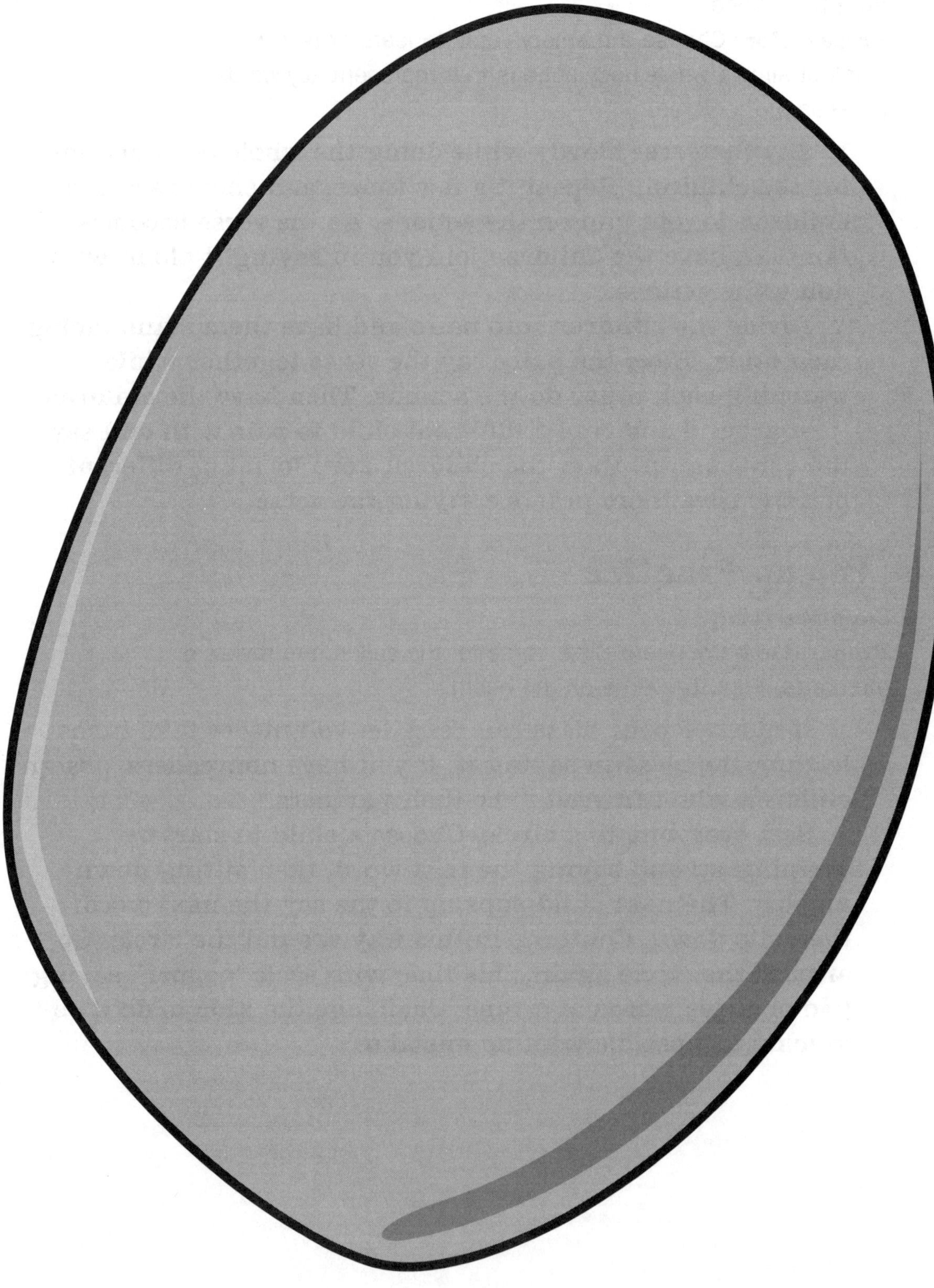

16. Signed Verse

Supplies: None

Preparation: Choose a Bible verse for the children to learn or review. Make up motions to represent key words in the verse. You might choose to use American Sign Language instead. Check your local library or Internet sites for help in finding basic signs.

First show the children the motions (or signs) without words and see if they can guess what words the motions represent. Then say the verse with the motions. Say it again and have the children do the motions with you. Then have the whole class repeat the verse, along with the motions. For extra practice, split into pairs, and have the pairs face each other while saying the verse with the motions.

17. Stepping-Stones

Supplies: Paper, marker, (optional: scissors, masking tape)

Preparation: Before class divide the verse into manageable phrases and print these phrases on separate sheets of paper. You may cut the papers into a stepping-stone shapes. Make enough sets of the stepping-stones so that the children can be in groups of four or five. Select a Bible verse that you would like the children to memorize today.

Divide the children into groups. Each group begins by placing their stepping-stones, in order, in the shape of a path. Depending on your space, the children may spread out their paths or even cross paths with other groups' stepping-stones. The children in each group line up at the beginning of their path, and take turns walking the path. The children say the words on each stepping-stone as they step on it. Note: If your floor is slippery, either tape down the stones or have the children step next to them for safety reasons.

After each child has had a turn, let the children turn over a few of their stepping-stones and repeat the activity, seeing who can walk the path and say the verse correctly.

18. Team Tag

Supplies: Paper, marker

Preparation: Print or type each phrase of the verse on a separate sheet of paper. Make one set of verse phrases for every five to six children. For the sets that preschoolers will use, add pictures to represent the phrases.

Say the verse for the children phrase by phrase, and have them repeat it after you. Do this a few times. Then divide the children into groups of five or six. Each small group sits in a circle and places a set of mixed-up verse phrases in the center. Designate one child as the beginner. That child says the first phrase and then finds the paper with that phrase on it. Another child says the second phrase and gets it from the pile. A third child gets the third phrase. Once all the phrases have been said and retrieved, have the groups lay their papers down in order. Let the groups mix up the papers and repeat the game for the rest of your allotted time.

19. Traveling Verse

Supplies: Chalkboard or whiteboard, chalk or whiteboard marker, eraser

Preparation: Choose a memory verse that supports the lesson. Print the verse on the board. If you have nonreaders in your group, draw a small picture above each of the key words to represent it.

Read the verse aloud in unison, slowly, a few times. Point to each word as it is read. Then travel, as a group, to another place of the classroom and say the verse together. Move the group to a second place and say the verse together. Repeat moving and saying the verse until the group can say the verse without looking at the board.

20. Verse Relay

Supplies: None

Preparation: Choose a Bible verse for the children to memorize. It may be one they've worked on before.

Say the Bible verse, phrase by phrase, and have the children repeat it after you. When the children are familiar with it, divide the children into teams of four or five players. Have each team line up. At your signal, each team will "pass" the memory verse down their team line: The first child turns and says the verse to the second child. That child turns and says the verse to the third child, and so on. Each child must say it correctly before the next child can turn and pass it along. The team that correctly passes the verse to the end of the line first is the winner. Play again as time permits.

21. Verse Scramble

Supplies: None

Preparation: Choose a Bible verse that supports the day's lesson.

Pick two or three key words from the verse. Have the children listen carefully as you say the verse. Ask them to raise a hand whenever you say one of the key words. Repeat the verse a few times, encouraging the children to say the key words along with you as they remember them. Then challenge the children to say whole phrases of the verse with you.

Once the children know the verse, divide them into groups of three. Say the verse all together. As soon as you've said the reference, have the kids scramble to get in different groups. Again say the verse and have the kids scramble afterward. Continue until the kids have been in several groups and all know the verse.

22. Verse Walking Game

Supplies: None

Preparation: Select a Bible verse to learn or review.

Say the verse with the class a few times. Then divide the children into two groups, and have them line up on opposite sides of the room, facing each other. Explain to the children they will become a "walking verse"—each group will say the verse in unison as they walk to the opposite side of the classroom. They may not touch another person as they walk, even though they will be passing through the line of the group opposite them. Students may walk only when they are saying the Bible verse. If they need to think about what comes next in the verse, they have to stop while they think.

The children may need to repeat the Bible verse a few times before reaching the other side, depending on how slowly they walk. Give the signal and have the kids do the "Verse Walk." If time permits have the teams turn around and play again.

23. Verse Waves

Supplies: None

Preparation: Write the Bible memory verse on the board.

Say the verse phrase by phrase, and have the children repeat it after you. Repeat the verse until the verse is familiar to the kids. Then have the children form a circle. Choose a child to begin by saying only the first word of the memory verse. The child to the right says the second word of the verse. Continue going around the circle, with each child saying only the next word of the verse. As the children learn the verse, they will be able to go faster and the verse will sound more natural.

Next have all the children squat down (still in the circle). This time as each child says their word, they spring up with their arms up, and then quickly stoop back down again. As they go around the circle the waving arms will look like an ocean wave. Repeat the verse this way a few times.

Notes

Notes

Ball, Balloon, and Beanbag Games

Note: Use balloon games with elementary children and older. Balloons can be a choking hazard for younger children. Keep balloons away from faces.

1. Balloon Batting

Supplies: Balloon (inflated)

Preparation: Choose a Bible verse to learn or review.

Practice the verse with the class several times by saying each phrase and having the children repeat it after you. Then have the children stand in a large circle. One child gently hits the balloon across the circle, saying the first word of the verse. The child who hits the balloon next says the second word of the verse. The third child says the third word, and so on. Encourage the children to bat the balloon to children who have not yet had a turn so that all may take part.

When the whole verse has been said, play again, this time using phrases of the verse instead of individual words. Repeat the game as time permits. When finished, pop the balloon and have the class recite the verse together.

2. Balloons in the Air

Supplies: An inflated balloon for each student. You may want to have extras.

Preparation: Choose a memory verse that supports the lesson. Keep the inflated balloons in a large trash bag until ready to use.

Say the verse aloud in unison, slowly, a few times. Give each child a balloon. Then say the verse together as a class. Have the children tap their balloons in the air each time they say a word. Provide new balloons when balloons pop. Remind all of the children to say the verse.

Once the children know the verse, you could have them take turns saying the verse alone rather than with the whole class.

3. Balloon Mix-up

Supplies: Balloons, permanent ink marker
Preparation: Inflate one balloon for each word in the chosen
Bible verse. Write one word of the verse on each balloon with a
permanent ink marker.

Say the Bible Verse several times with the children before playing the game.

Place the prepared balloons in a central area. Show the kids where they will line up to put the balloons in order. Have the kids, one at a time, come up and pick any balloon. That child reads the word on the balloon and then stands in line near where that word should go in the verse. You may need to help nonreaders "read" the word on their balloon and figure out where to stand. Continue until all the balloons are placed in the correct order. Then have the children read the verse together. If you have more balloons than children, let the kids simply place their balloons on the floor in the proper spot in line. As time permits, mix up the balloons and play again.

4. Balloon Verse Pass

Supplies: Balloon (inflated)
Preparation: Choose a Bible verse for the children to memorize or review.

Say the verse phrase by phrase and have the class repeat each phrase after you. Then have the children stand in a circle. Give the balloon to one child to start. That child says the first word of the verse and begins to pass the balloon around the circle. Each child says the next word of the verse. Allow the children to pass slowly until they become confident with the verse. Then encourage them to pass more quickly so that the verse is said at normal speed.

If the children are confident with the verse you chose, let them bat the balloon across the circle rather than passing it, or let them say verse phrases rather than individual words.

5. Beanbag Toss

Supplies: Beanbag (one per group of six or fewer kids)

Preparation: Choose a Bible verse to learn or review. Clearly print the verse on a chalkboard or whiteboard.

Begin to teach the verse to the class by reading it slowly while pointing to each word. Repeat the verse several times, encouraging the children to join you as they begin to remember it. The repetition and pointing will help nonreaders.

When the verse is familiar to the children, divide the class into groups of about four to six children each. The group sizes don't need to be identical.

Each group forms a circle and tosses the beanbag randomly around the circle. Whoever catches the beanbag says a word of the verse and then tosses it to another child, who says the next word, and so on. Let the children refer to the board if they can't remember the next word.

As the children become familiar with the verse, make it more challenging by having groups compete against each other to see which team can work through the entire verse the fastest without a mistake.

6. Bible Verse Volleyball

Supplies: Masking tape, inflated balloons

Preparation: Choose a Bible verse to learn or review. Place a line down the middle of your game area with masking tape.

Divide the children into two equal teams, and have one team stand on each side of the line.

Begin by repeating the memory verse together several times. If it is new to the children, say the verse phrase by phrase and have the children say it after you. Then begin the game: Give the balloon to one team. One player bats it across the line while their whole team calls out the first phrase. A player on the opposite team bats the balloon back while that whole team calls out the second phrase. The first team bats the balloon again while saying the next phrase. Continue playing until the whole verse has been said. See how long the teams can keep the volley going and how many times in a row they can say the verse without mistakes.

If the verse is short, you may have the teams call one
word at a time rather than phrases. Play with only one
balloon, but have more on hand in case one pops.

7. Hot Potato

Supplies: A beanbag or soft ball

Preparation: Choose a Bible verse to learn or review.

Have the children sit in a circle. Say the verse for them, pausing after each phrase to let the children repeat it after you. Repeat the verse a few times, then begin the memory game.

Give the beanbag (the "potato") to one child to start passing around the circle. As each child touches the beanbag, the whole class says one word of the memory verse. Start out slowly to give the children a chance to remember all the words (you may tell them the "potato" is not hot yet). As the verse is repeated a few times and the beanbag continues around the circle, the children will find themselves memorizing the verse. At this point, you may wish to switch to having the individual children say the words of the verse as they pass the beanbag. Play until the beanbag can be passed and the verse said smoothly and quickly—while the potato is "hot."

8. Music Ball

Supplies: Beanbag or soft ball, CD, and CD player

Preparation: Choose a Bible verse to learn or review.

Begin by saying the verse phrase by phrase and having the children repeat it after you. Then ask the kids to form a circle to play "Music Ball." The kids pass a beanbag or ball around the circle while you play a song on the CD player. When the music stops, whoever is holding the ball or beanbag tries to say the verse from memory. Players that say it right get to work the CD player for the next round of play. Continue as long as time permits so that most of the children have a chance to say the verse.

You could also set this up in two circles if you have a large number of children.

9. Tic-Tac-Toe

Supplies: Masking tape, eight beanbags of two different colors (optional: sidewalk chalk)

Preparation: Use masking tape to make a tic-tac-toe grid on the floor, about 3' x 3'. If the weather is nice, you may want to draw the grid outside with sidewalk chalk. If your class is large, make more than one grid. Choose a Bible verse for the children to memorize.

Divide the children into two teams, and assign each team a color of beanbag. A child on one team tosses the beanbag and says the memory verse. If the verse is said correctly, the beanbag stays in that square. If the verse is incorrect, the beanbag is picked up. Then a child from the other team tosses a beanbag and says the verse. Again, if the verse is correct, that beanbag stays.

If the children are unfamiliar with the verse, for the first round of play you may let the whole team or any child on a team say the verse. Play several rounds to give the children more practice reciting the verse.

10. Word Toss

Supplies: Poster board, marker, beanbags or other items that can be tossed (chalkboard erasers, paper wads, etc.)

Preparation: Choose a Bible verse for today's memory activity. Print the memory verse in large letters on a sheet of poster board, putting space between the words.

Place the prepared poster board on the floor, and have the children gather around it. Read the verse together several times. Then have all the kids take two or three giant steps backward. Hand out the beanbags to a few children. The kids take turns tossing their beanbag onto the poster board from wherever they are standing. Whichever word of the memory verse their beanbag lands on (or nearest), that child says the memory verse starting with that word. Initially, the children may read the verse from the poster board. Once the children begin to learn the verse, have them try to say it without looking. Let different children retrieve the beanbags and have a turn.

Notes

Chalkboard or Whiteboard Games

S _____ O _____

A _____

I L _____ ,

GALATIANS 5:13

1. Category Memory Game

Supplies: Chalkboard or whiteboard, chalk or whiteboard marker, eraser

Preparation: Choose a verse to learn or review. Write the verse on the board.

Read the verse with the class while pointing to each word. Repeat it several times. Then call out different categories that suit your class, such as clothing color or pattern, hair color, boys, girls, age, and so on. Whichever category you call, the kids who fit that group stand and say the verse together. Allow groups to read the verse from the board for help several times, then erase some or all of the verse as you go along.

2. Echo Verse

Supplies: Chalkboard or whiteboard, chalk or whiteboard marker

Preparation: Choose a Bible verse for the children to learn or review. Write the Bible verse on the board but divide it into small segments or phrases.

Divide the children into two groups. Have them sit on opposite sides of the room facing each other. Begin by calling out a segment or phrase of the verse and having the whole class echo you. Continue until the entire verse has been echoed. Then repeat the verse, this time having one of the groups do the calling while the second group echoes. On the third practice, have the second group call the segments and the first group echo them.

3. Erase-a-Word

Supplies: Chalkboard or whiteboard, chalk or whiteboard marker, eraser

Preparation: Choose a memory verse that supports the lesson. Print the verse on the board. If you have nonreaders in your group, draw a small picture above each of the key words to represent it.

Read the verse aloud in unison, slowly, a few times. Point to each word as it is read. Then erase one word with its picture, and read the verse again in unison, including the missing word. Play a game to further learn the verse. Erase another word, and read the verse again. Continue erasing words and repeating the verse until the class can say the verse without any words or pictures to help them.

4. Every Single Word

Supplies: Chalkboard or whiteboard, chalk or whiteboard marker, eraser

Preparation: Choose a new verse to memorize or continue practicing a verse the children need to review. Write the verse on the board.

Read the verse aloud for the class. Then explain that to practice it, children will take turns reading it and putting the emphasis on a different word. The first child reads it, emphasizing the first word of the verse (saying it more loudly). The next child says the whole verse, emphasizing only the second word. The third child emphasizes the third word. Continue this way until every word has been emphasized.

Start with kids who are good readers to give nonreaders time to start memorizing the verse. You could also have everyone say the verse each time and add the emphasis.

5. Letter-by-Letter

Supplies: Chalkboard or whiteboard, chalk or whiteboard marker, eraser

Preparation: Choose a Bible verse for the children to learn or review. Write the fist letter of each word of the Bible verse on the board. Behind the first letter write a blank for each letter of the word.

Play a game as the children try to figure out the words. Begin with the first word and let the children guess letters one at a time. If they guess the wrong letter, write that letter in a "Wrong Letter" word bank. If they guess the right letter, write the letter on the blank. Continue to guess each word in order. Encourage the children to go back and read the completed words to help them figure out the new word. When they have guessed the whole verse, repeat it together a few times.

6. Letter Clues

Supplies: Chalkboard or whiteboard, chalk or whiteboard marker, eraser

Preparation: Select a Bible verse to review or reinforce your lesson. Write the verse on the board and underline each word.

Lead the children in saying the verse in unison two or three times as you point to each word. Then erase all but the first letter of each word and the underlines. (You should now have only the first letter of each word and a blank after it, such as, t_____.) Point to each blank as you repeat the verse a couple more times. Then erase the remaining letters, leaving the blanks. Point to the blanks as you say the verse together again.

7. Star Verse

Supplies: Chalkboard or whiteboard, chalk or whiteboard marker, eraser

Preparation: Choose a memory verse that supports the lesson. Print the verse on the board.

Read the verse aloud in unison, slowly, a few times. Point to each word as it is read. Then replace one word with a star, and read the verse again in unison, including the missing word. Play a game to further learn the verse. Erase another word, add a star, and read the verse again. Continue erasing words, adding stars, and repeating the verse until the class can say the verse with only stars on the board.

8. Verse Telephone

Supplies: Chalkboard or whiteboard, chalk or whiteboard marker, eraser

Preparation: Choose a memory verse that supports the lesson.

Have the class sit in a line with you at the beginning. Whisper the first word of the verse to the child sitting next to you. That child whispers the word to the next child. Continue whispering and passing the word to the end of the line. The child at the end of the line writes the word on the board, then moves to sit next to you. Repeat for each word until the entire verse is written on the board. Say the verse several times together.

9. Whisper 'n' Shout

Supplies: Chalkboard or whiteboard, chalk or whiteboard marker

Preparation: Choose a Bible verse the children have started learning or choose a new one. Write the verse on the board.

Read the verse slowly as you point to each word. Explain any words the children may not know. Then have the class start repeating the verse very softly and increase in volume. First, just mouth the words. Next, whisper very softly, then whisper loudly. Next, say the verse in a normal tone of voice, then loudly. Finally, have girls and boys face off and see if they can shout the verse to each other from memory.

Games That Don't Need Supplies

1. Animals' Good Memories

Supplies: None

Preparation: Choose a Bible verse that reinforces the unit theme of God's love, either one worked on in Sunday school or a new one.

Say each phrase of the verse clearly and have the class echo it after you. Repeat a few times until the verse is familiar to the children.

Divide the class into groups of three or four. Assign each group an animal that may have been on the ark, such as elephants, parrots, monkeys, horses, and so on. Allow a few minutes for each animal group to say the verse among themselves a few times.

Then have a contest to see which "animal" has the "best memory." Let each small group have a turn to stand and say the verse together. Keep the competition light-hearted and positive by having the groups encourage one another. **Those elephants have good memories! Is it because their brains are bigger? Let's see if the clever monkeys can remember the whole verse.**

When all groups have had a turn, congratulate the "animals."

2. Charade Verse

Supplies: None

Preparation: Choose a memory verse that supports the lesson. Try to choose a verse that lends itself to actions. Then think of full-body actions that represent key words or phrases of the verse, such as kneeling, reaching up high, patting another on the back and so on.

First, silently do the full-body actions for the children and see if they can guess what words you are motioning. As the children guess, tell them the specific words or phrases related to those actions. Then have the children imitate your actions while saying the words.

After guessing all the actions, have the children act out the verse while saying it together.

3. Echoing God's Word

Supplies: None

Preparation: Choose a Bible verse for the children to memorize. You could also use a verse they have worked on before.

Have the children practice the verse by repeating each phrase as an echo. Have the girls stand on one side of the classroom and the boys on the other. To begin, you call the verse phrases and have all the children echo you. Then have the boys call the verse and the girls echo it. Repeat the activity with the girls calling and the boys echoing.

Here is an example using Luke 2:11. Phrases to echo: A Savior / has been born / to you; / he is Christ / the Lord. / Luke 2:11

4. Echo Verse

Supplies: None

Preparation: Choose a Bible verse to learn or review.

Today we'll pretend that there is a large canyon between us. Whatever I say into the canyon, you echo back to me. Have the children stand on the other side of the room from you.

Begin by calling out the first word of the verse and having the whole class echo you. Continue until the entire verse has been echoed. Then repeat the verse, this time calling out phrases. Finally, call out the entire verse for the class to echo.

5. Good News Shout

Supplies: None

Preparation: Choose a verse that highlights the lesson theme. It may be a verse previously used, which you can reinforce, or a new verse.

Have the class stand and repeat each phrase of the verse as you say it. Each time you complete the verse and reference, shout, "That's good news!" Have the class join you as you shout. Repeat the verse and shout a few times.

Then have the class form two lines facing each other. One line says the verse together by memory, followed by both groups shouting together, "That's good news!" Then the other line says the verse in unison, again followed with the shout by both groups. You could have the groups do the shout in different volumes, such as from whispering to calling loudly, until everyone knows the verse.

6. Group and Regroup

Supplies: None

Preparation: Choose a Bible verse for the children to memorize or review.

Say the verse for the class, phrase by phrase, and have them repeat it after you. Do this a few times until the verse becomes familiar.

Then explain that you're going to name some groups and whoever fits in that group will stand and say the verse together. Call out groups like these: kids wearing green, all boys, kids who are seven years old, kids who have brothers, kids who like watermelon, kids who ate cereal for breakfast, or kids with brown hair.

Change the groups to fit your class, and try to choose groups that will bring at least two children to their feet. Add more until all the kids have had a chance to say the verse a few times.

Notes

Notes

Games with a Variety of Supplies

1. Coin Exchange

Supplies: Real or toy pennies (two for each child)
Preparation: Choose a memory verse for the class to work on. It may be a new one that supports the lesson focus or a review verse learned in Sunday school. Print the verse on the board for the children to refer to.

Read the verse together while pointing to each word to help nonreaders. Be sure all the kids understand what it means. Say the verse together a few more times.

Then give each child two coins. The kids walk around looking for someone to "give" both their money and the verse to in this manner: A child hands his coins to another child and says the verse. The other child reciprocates, so both children end up with money again. Then they both find another child to "give" to as they say the verse. Play for as long as time permits.

2. Concentration in the Stable

Supplies: Felt in dark brown and a light color, scissors, glue, marker, felt board
Preparation: Choose a Bible verse for the children to memorize or review. Copy the pictures of Bible-time animals on the following pages and cut them out. You will need one picture for each word in the verse. Trace each animal on a piece of felt; cut out the felt and glue it to the back of the animal picture. On the back of each felt animal, print one word from the Bible memory verse. Also cut out strips of dark brown felt to make the outline of a stable.

Set up the felt board, and place the felt stable outline on it. Say the memory verse for the children slowly, holding up each prepared felt animal as you say the word on its back. Don't place the animals in the stable yet. Then say the verse again, inviting the children to say it with you. Now let volunteers come up and place each animal in the stable in order, reading the word on its back as they do so.

Once all the animals are in the stable, see who can remember which animals have which words on them, in the right order. If a child picks a word in the wrong order, he or she should make the sound of the animal instead. Play a few times until the children know the verse.

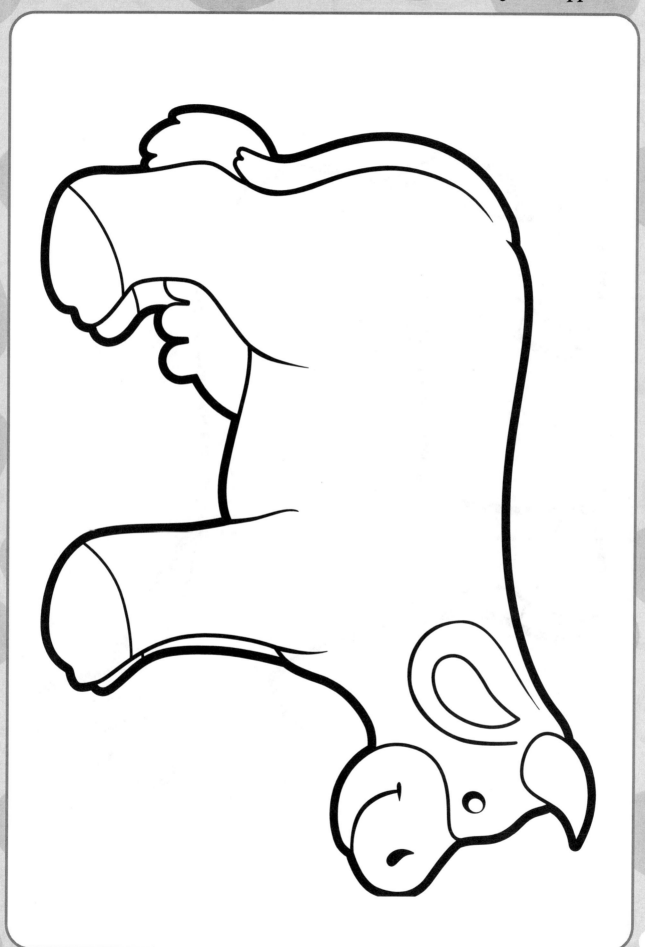

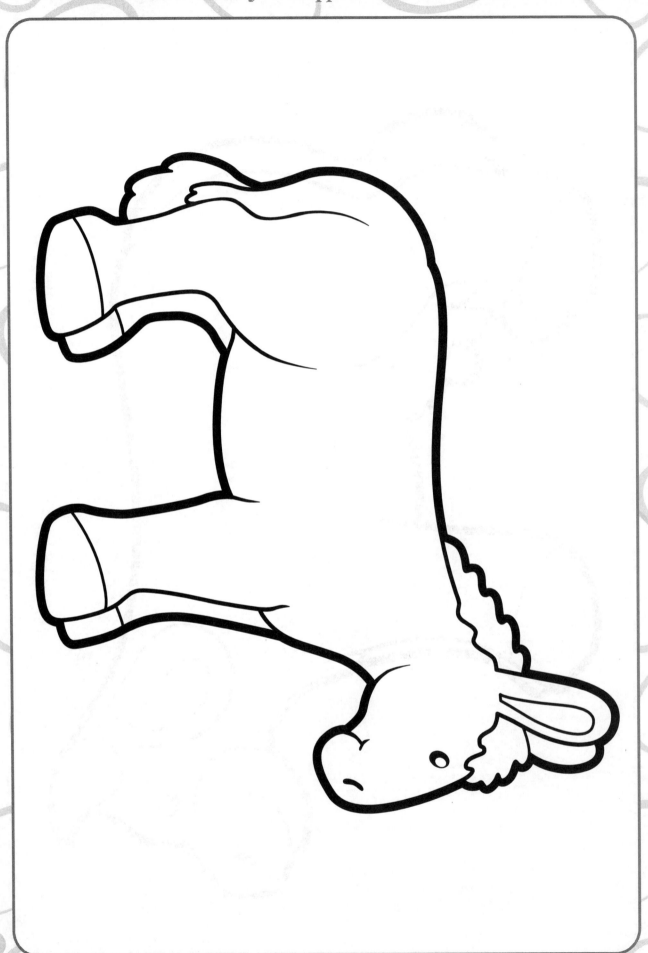

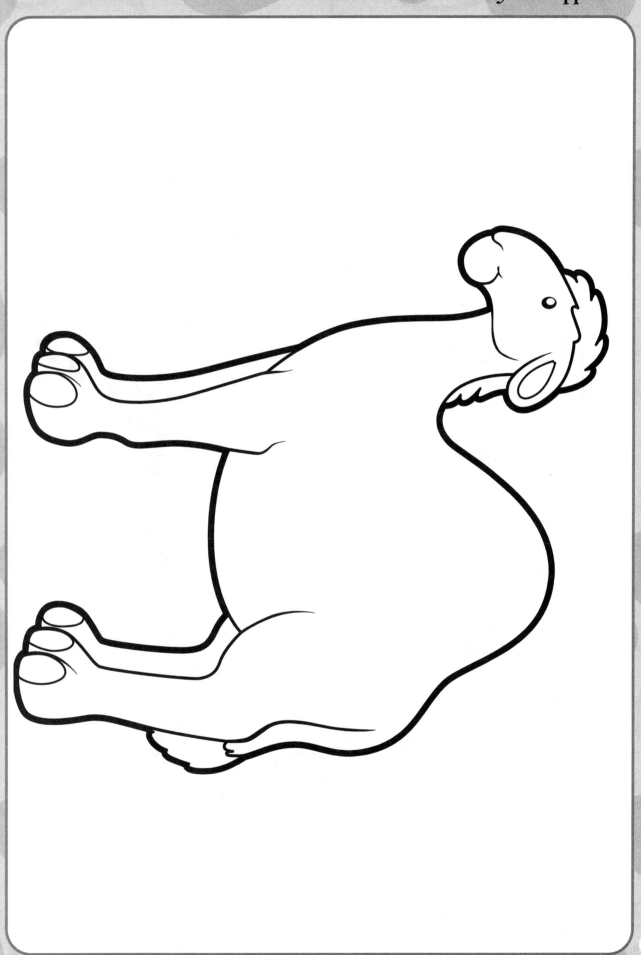

3. Fish in the Net

Supplies: Construction paper, scissors, marker, net bag (such as for produce or laundry)

Preparation: Decide on a Bible memory verse that highlights the lesson. Cut simple fish shapes from construction paper. Print one word or phrase of the verse on each, adding a simple picture or symbol where appropriate to help nonreaders. Place the fish in a net bag. If you have a large group of children, you might want to make two sets of fish and place them in separate net bags.

Practice the verse with the class by saying portions of it and having the class repeat it after you. Repeat until the verse is familiar to the children.

Then have children take turns coming up and taking a fish out of the net. Once all the fish are taken, ask the kids to gather on the floor and work together to put the words in proper order. When completed, read the verse together again. If you are using two bags of fish, have the groups work on this activity simultaneously.

4. Pass the Basket

Supplies: Baby doll, basket or box for the doll to fit in

Preparation: Choose a Bible verse for the children to memorize. You could either review a verse or introduce a new one.

With the children seated in a circle, say the verse phrase by phrase, and have the children repeat it after you. Explain any unfamiliar words. Say the verse several times and have the children join you as they remember it.

Give the baby doll in the basket to one child to start. Explain that this doll is like baby Moses and they are sitting along the banks of the Nile River. The children will say the Bible verse together while gently pushing baby Moses along the Nile to the next child. As the children learn it, switch to individual children saying a phrase of the verse in order as each one passes it.

5. Pass the Phone

Supplies: Cell phone or child's play phone

Preparation: Choose a Bible verse for the children to memorize. It may be one learned in Sunday school or another verse that supports the lesson theme.

Have the children sit in a line. Hold the cell phone or play phone to your ear and say the memory verse, pretending to be talking into the phone. Hand the phone to the first child and have him or her say the verse into the phone. Then that child passes the phone to the next child in line. Each child passes the phone to the next child to say the verse into the phone. The last child says the verse and then begins passing the phone back up the line, with each child saying the verse again. Keep passing the phone and repeating the verse until the children know it well.

6. Planting Memory Seeds

Supplies: Dried lima beans, several for each child; paper; glue

Preparation: Select a memory verse that reviews a verse the children have been learning in Sunday school or a new one. Place glue bottles at a few spots around the room where children can stop and use it.

Say the memory verse for the class, phrase by phrase, and have the kids repeat it after you. Check to make sure the children understand all the words. Repeat the verse a few more times so it becomes familiar to the children.

Give each child several beans and a piece of paper. (Watch to be sure children are not trying to eat the beans.) The children move around the room looking for others to practice saying the memory verse to. Each time a child says the verse, he receives a bean from the child he said it to. The kids need to take turns listening to and practicing saying the verse so that the seeds are fairly evenly distributed. After every two or three beans, the children may pause to put tiny dots of glue on their paper and add the newly collected beans. Then the kids return to finding more kids to say the verse to and collecting more beans to glue.

7. String-a-Verse

Supplies: Colorful O-shaped cereal, string or yarn
Preparation: Choose a Bible verse for the children to memorize or review. Cut a necklace-length piece of string or yarn for each child. Tie a knot in one end. Place the cereal in bowls.

Say the memory verse phrase by phrase, and have the children repeat it after you. Then give each child a necklace-length piece of string or yarn. Place the cereal bowls where all can reach it. Let the children add one piece of cereal to their string for each word in the verse as they say it aloud.

Extend the activity by having children reverse the process and remove a cereal bead as the verse is said. Then the children can restring the necklace while saying the verse a third time. Tie the ends of each necklace together. Keep the necklaces in a separate place until the end of class.

As children leave, encourage them to say the Bible verse as they eat their necklaces.

8. Stuffed Animal Pass

Supplies: Three cuddly stuffed animals
Preparation: Choose a Bible verse to learn or review. Plan an easy way to divide the verse into three segments.

Do you ever hug a stuffed animal? We'll use these stuffed animals to help us learn the verse today. Say the first third of the verse while holding up the first stuffed animal. Have a helper hold up the second animal while you say the second portion of the verse. Have another helper hold up the third animal while you say the last part of the verse. Now repeat the process, pausing to let the children echo you after each portion. Do it a few times so that the children associate the three different stuffed animals with the three parts of the verse.

Then ask the children to sit in a circle. Hand the animals to three children seated beside one other. Let them each say the portion of the verse (in order) that goes with the animal they are holding. Then the children pass the stuffed animals to the next child, and those three say their parts of the verse. Continue passing the animals around the circle and repeating the verse until everyone has had a turn.

9. Treasure Hunt

Supplies: Small toys or objects that relate to words in the chosen Bible verse.

Preparation: Choose a Bible verse to learn or review. Collect small toys or objects that can be used to represent words in the Bible verse. Hide the toys or objects throughout the room before children arrive.

Tell the verse to the children a phrase at a time. Have the children repeat each phrase back to you. Repeat the verse several times.

Ask the children to help each other find objects hidden throughout the room that have to do with the Bible verse. You may want to tell them how many objects they need to find.

Give a signal and let the kids find the cards. Make sure every child finds at least one object. Then have the children work together to put the objects in verse order. When completed, have the class say the verse together as you point to the objects.

10. Verse Recordings

Supplies: Cassette recorder and blank tape, chalkboard and chalk

Preparation: Choose a Bible verse for the children to memorize or review. Print the memory verse on the board where all can see it.

Divide the children into small groups. You may want to have helpers in the groups. The small groups should practice saying the verse until they feel comfortable with it. Then let the groups take turns recording themselves saying the verse into a tape recorder. After each group has recorded the verse, play back the tape for all to listen to.

11. Yarn Connections

Supplies: Balls of yarn, wrapped so that they unroll easily
Preparation: Choose a memory verse that supports the lesson
or reviews another verse previously memorized.

Say the verse phrase by phrase, and have the class repeat
it after you. Do this a few times.

Divide the class into groups of about eight kids each. Give
each group a ball of yarn. The first person with the yarn
says the first word of the verse, then holds the loose end of
the yarn and tosses the rest of the ball to someone across the
circle. The child who catches the ball says the second word,
keeps hold of the yarn thread, and tosses the ball to someone
else. As the children continue tossing the yarn (saying a
word of the verse on each toss), a crisscross pattern will
form across the circle. Encourage the groups to "stay con-
nected" by holding the yarn strings taut and saying the
verse correctly.

Notes

Notes

Games with Puppets

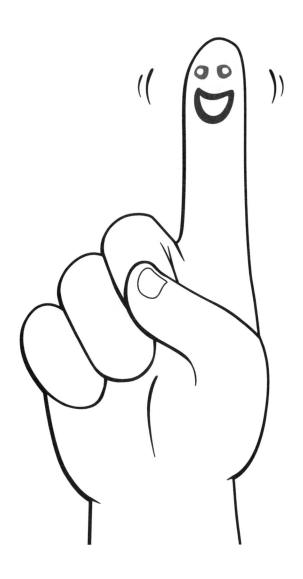

1. Finger Faces

Supplies: Washable markers, (optional: disposable wipes)
Preparation: Choose a Bible verse for the children to learn or review.

Use a washable marker to draw eyes and a mouth on one fingertip of each child. The children can make their finger face "talk" as they wiggle it. Divide the children into pairs, and let them make their finger faces say the verse to one another. You could also have the children walk around the room and make their finger faces repeat the verse to whomever they see. Encourage accuracy in saying the verse, even as they are having fun.

Provide wipes for children to clean off their fingers when the activity is done.

2. Helper Tickets

Supplies: Index cards or slips of construction paper, hand puppets

Preparation: Choose a Bible verse for the children to memorize. It may be one already learned or a new verse that supports the lesson.

Say the verse for the class, phrase by phrase, and have them repeat it after you. Be sure the children understand the meaning of the verse. Say it together a few more times until it becomes familiar.

Give each child a few index cards or slips of paper, and explain that these are "helper tickets" that will allow them to ask for help. The children are to mill around the room and stop by any friend. The two of them say the verse to each other. Then they wander further, stop someone else, and say the verse again. They do this repeatedly for your allotted time. But whenever a child gets stuck or needs help saying the verse, the child calls over a hand puppet and gives him or her a "ticket"—this allows the puppet to coach them through that spot of the verse.

Get the children started, and encourage a fun atmosphere of finding a friend and trying to say the verse.

3. Lined-Up Words

Supplies: Index cards, pen, hand puppet

Preparation: Choose a Bible verse for the children to memorize. In large, clear letters, print each word of the verse on an index card. Keep the cards in order.

Use the hand puppet to "learn" the verse along with the children. Have the puppet take the first index card and hold it up. Lead the class in reading it aloud. Repeat with all the cards.

Then let the puppet give out the index cards to the children. Let the children with cards come to the front and arrange themselves in the correct order. Have all the children, led by the puppet, read the verse together. Let the children give their cards to other children and play again.

4. Microphone Verse

Supplies: Boom box or karaoke machine with microphone, hand puppets

Preparation: Choose a memory verse that supports the lesson or that reviews a verse the children learned earlier.

Say the verse to the class while speaking into the microphone. Let the hand puppets take turns saying the verse into the microphone as well. They should encourage the children to join in as they begin to remember the verse.

Ask for volunteers to take turns saying the verse into the microphone. Try to let every child have a turn.

5. Pass-the-Verse Relay

Supplies: A hand puppet for every six to eight children, one helper for each group

Preparation: Choose a Bible verse for children to learn or review.

Say the verse with the children, and be sure they understand all the words. Then say the verse phrase by phrase a few times, having the class repeat each phrase after you.

Divide the class into teams of six to eight players each plus a helper. Have the teams line up. The last child in each line should hold a hand puppet. Each line will "pass" the verse from child to child until the child with the puppet says the verse. See which line can say the verse both correctly and quickly. The helper in each group can be sure that the children are "passing" the verse correctly. They can assist the children as necessary to keep things moving.

You may begin by having the kids pass the verse phrase by phrase. At the end of each round, the children pass the puppets to the kids standing in front of them and move to the front of the line. After a couple of rounds, let each child say the whole verse before "passing" it to the next child. Emphasize that accuracy is more important than speed, and encourage supportive words among teammates.

6. Puppet Competition

Supplies: Two hand puppets, two volunteers

Preparation: Choose a Bible verse. You can use a previously learned verse or introduce a new one.

Use two hand puppets, each worked by a volunteer, to help the kids practice. Divide the class into two groups, with a puppet for each. Say something like, **Today we're going to have a little competition. These puppets both think they can help you learn the verse, so each will help one group. After they've helped you learn the verse, we'll come back together and see if they can prove that they were good verse teachers.**

Send each group to a different part of the room, and allow several minutes for them to work on memorizing. When you call them back together, have each puppet lead its group in saying the verse. Lead each group in applauding for the other when done.

7. Share Your Help

Supplies: Several index cards, a hand puppet

Preparation: Choose a memory verse that supports the lesson or reviews a verse learned earlier. Write the verse on each index card.

Explain that the children will learn the verse today by sharing with one another. Divide the kids into small groups, making sure there are nonreaders mixed with older children, if applicable. Give each group an index card with the verse on it. Older kids can "share" their reading ability by reading the verse to the group several times. Younger kids can "share" their cooperation and "being smart" by listening hard and trying to remember the words. Encourage the kids to work together in learning the verse.

As kids begin to have the verse memorized, they may go up to a hand puppet (worked by you or a helper) and "share" the verse with it. Allow all the children to have a turn.

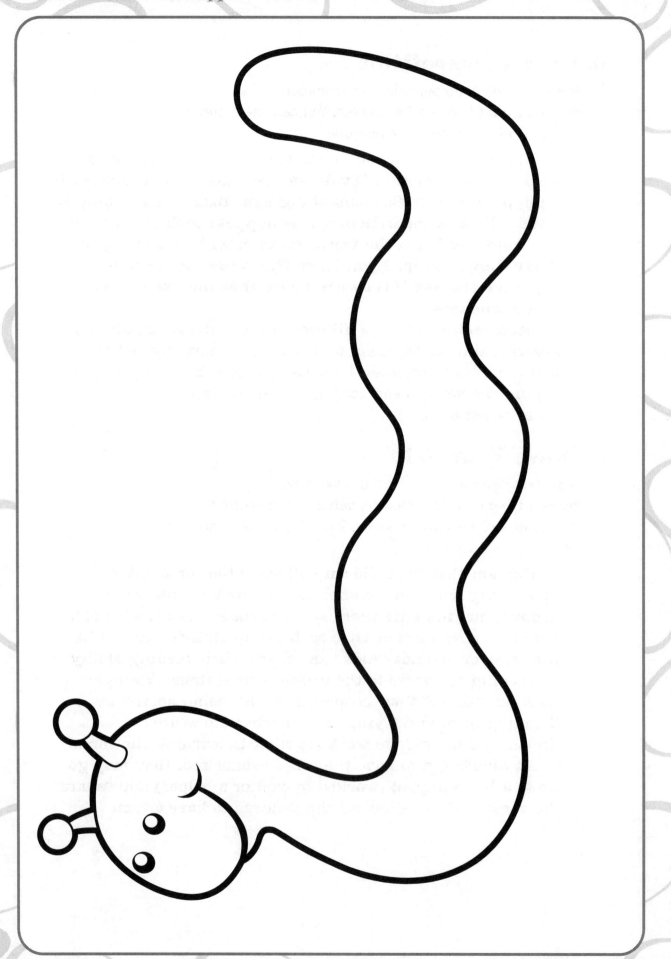

8. Wiggly Worms

Supplies: Poster board, marker, scissors, bird puppet or toy bird

Preparation: Choose a memory verse. Print the verse in large letters on poster board. Cut each word or phrase into the shape of a wiggly worm. (See pattern on page 76.) If your class is large, make two or more sets of verse worms.

Put the verse worms on the floor, and have the children gather around. Read the verse aloud slowly, and let the children find the words or phrases on the worms and place them in order.

Read the verse together two or three times. Then have the bird puppet "eat" one of the worms (pick it up and remove it). Read the verse in unison again, including the missing words. Let the bird eat another worm, and repeat the verse. Continue until all worms are gone. Then have the class say the verse from memory.

Notes

Music and Rhythm Games

1. Instrumental Rhythmic Verse

Supplies: Rhythm instruments

Preparation: Choose a Bible verse to teach or review. Think of a way to naturally repeat the verse in a rhythm. Practice saying the verse in rhythm, emphasizing the beats.

Say the Bible memory verse for the class in rhythm. Play a rhythm instrument, such as sticks or a maraca, to help the kids pick up on the downbeats. Repeat and have the children pat their laps as they listen. Repeat it a few times to help the children start remembering it.

Give out rhythm instruments, and let the kids play them in rhythm as they say the verse along with you. Repeat several times. When the verse is familiar, divide the class in half. Have one half say the verse while the other plays instruments. Then switch roles.

2. Musical Chairs Verse

Supplies: Chairs, CD, and CD player

Preparation: Choose a Bible verse to learn or review. Set up chairs for a game of "Musical Chairs." There should be one less chair than the number of children playing. The chairs should face outward in a circle or line.

Review the verse with the children a few times by having them repeat each phrase after you.

Softly play the music on the CD and have the whole group walk around the circle of chairs while saying the memory verse in unison. When the music stops, the kids quickly try to sit in a seat. The child left without a chair says the memory verse alone or with your help. Continue to play until the class is familiar with the verse.

3. Musical Groups

Supplies: Chairs, CD, and CD player
Preparation: Choose a Bible verse to learn or review.

Review the verse with the children a few times by having them repeat each phrase after you.

Softly play the music on the CD and have the whole group walk around the room. When the music stops, say a small number. The kids quickly form groups of that number and say the Bible verse to each other. Repeat playing and forming groups until the class is familiar with the verse.

4. Musical Memory Verse

Supplies: None
Preparation: Choose a Bible verse that supports the lesson or use this activity to review a memory verse. Think of a familiar tune that would fit the verse. Plan to teach the verse using that melody. Some ideas are "Row, Row, Row Your Boat," "Mary Had a Little Lamb," "Are You Sleeping?" "Twinkle, Twinkle, Little Star," or "London Bridge Is Falling Down."

Teach the memory verse by singing it for the children with the tune you chose. Sing it several times, and invite the children to join in on the parts they remember. As it becomes familiar, divide the class in half and have each half sing every other line to each other. End by singing the whole verse in unison a couple of times.

5. Musical Verse Mix

Supplies: Colored paper, CD, and CD player

Preparation: Choose a Bible verse to learn or review. Divide the verse into four sections and write each section on a separate piece of colored paper. Be sure to include the reference on one of the cards.

Say the Bible verse several times with the children. Arrange the children in a circle and hand out each paper to different sides of the circle after mixing up the order of the verse papers. Have the children pass the papers clockwise around the circle while you play a song from the CD. Stop the music after they have had time to pass the papers. The children holding the papers when the music stops move to the middle of the circle and put the words in the right order. Let them read the verse aloud and others in the circle repeat the verse back to them. They return to their places to begin again.

6. Pass the Crown

Supplies: Toy or paper crown (See page 83.), CD, and CD player

Preparation: Choose a Bible verse to learn or review.

Say the verse a few times, and have the children repeat each phrase after you. Make sure the children understand the meaning of the verse.

Have the children stand in a circle. Give one child the crown. Play a song from the CD. As the music plays, the children pass the crown around the circle. Stop the music at random. Whoever is holding the crown gets to say the verse. If the children are not yet sure of the verse, have the child holding the crown plus the child on either side of him or her say the verse together. Play for as long as time allows to give more children a chance to say the verse.

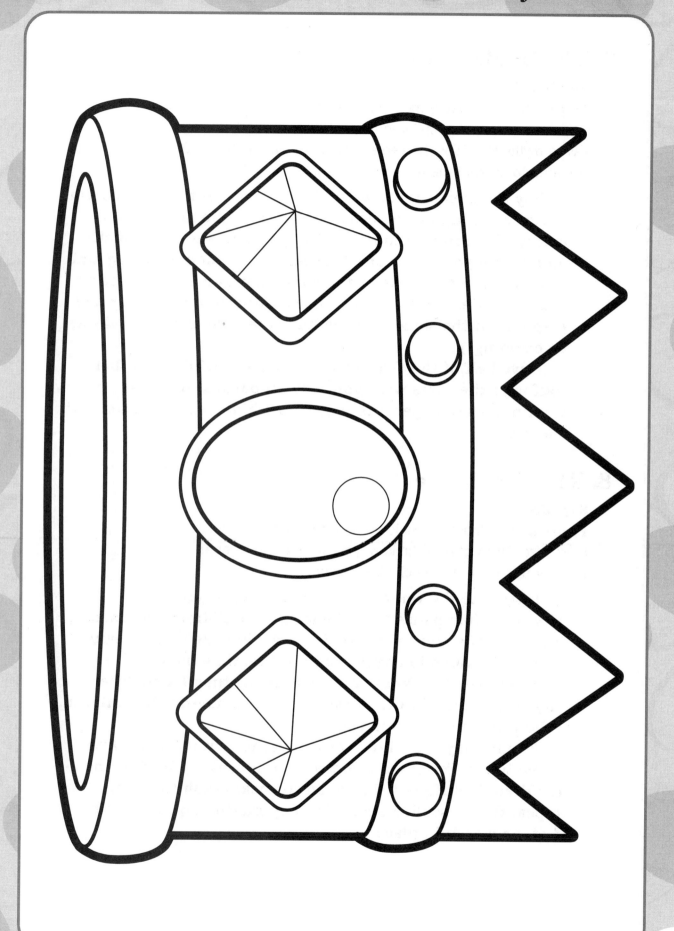

7. Rhythmic Verse

Supplies: None

Preparation: Choose a memory verse that supports the lesson or reviews a verse the children have already learned. Think of a way to rhythmically say the verse. Add claps on the beats. Be prepared to present the rhythmic verse in class.

Say the memory verse for the children in the rhythm you chose, clapping on the beats. Say it a couple more times, asking the children to listen for the beats and clap quietly along with you. Then ask the children to stop clapping and say with you the parts of the verse they remember. (Young children often have a hard time coordinating speaking and clapping at the same time, so have them do either speaking or clapping.)

Have half of the class clap the rhythm while the other half says the verse with you. Switch parts and repeat. Continue as time permits to give the kids more practice with the verse.

8. Rhythm Verse

Supplies: None

Preparation: Choose a Bible verse for the children to memorize. Think of a rhythmic way to say the Bible verse. Learn it to present to the children in class.

Introduce the verse to the children by saying it in rhythm. Then pause to make sure the children understand all the words and to briefly discuss what the verse means.

Say the verse in rhythm again, this time having the children pat their knees on the beats as they listen. Then say each phrase of the verse in rhythm, having the children echo it in rhythm after you.

Finally, say the whole verse together with the children a few times. For extra practice, you might try having the children do different things on the beats each time you repeat the verse. For example, they might clap, tap their feet, or march in place.

9. Set the Verse to Music

Supplies: Photocopies of the verse

Preparation: Choose a Bible verse to review.

Divide the children into groups of two or three. Give each group a copy of the verse. Have each group set the words to the music of a familiar tune or a rhythm. The groups will need to be spaced far apart as they work. Bring all the groups back together after a few minutes to perform a verse concert.

10. Verse Concert

Supplies: Rhythm instruments

Preparation: Choose a Bible verse to learn or review. Think of a way to say the memory verse in rhythm or to a beat.

Say the memory verse in rhythm for the children and have them listen carefully. Then let them pat their knees as you say it again. Next, say the verse phrase by phrase, in rhythm, and have the children echo it, also in rhythm. Repeat this a few times.

When the verse becomes familiar to the children, pass out rhythm instruments, and let the children give a "verse concert." They say the verse in unison as they play their instruments on the beats. For added practice, you could divide the children into two orchestras and let them take turns giving a verse concert for each other.

11. Verse Rap

Supplies: None

Preparation: Choose a Bible verse for the children to memorize. Figure out a way to say the verse with a bouncy rhythm or simple rap.

Say the memory verse for the children using the rhythm or rap you made up. Let the kids listen to it a few times before joining in. Once the children have practiced it together and feel confident, let the girls perform the verse rap for the boys, and then the boys for the girls.

Notes

Paper Games

God is our refuge and strength,

an ever-present help in trouble.

Psalm 46:1

God is our refuge and strength,

an ever-present help in trouble.

Psalm 46:1

1. Bible Verse Stairway

Supplies: Construction paper, marker, masking tape

Preparation: Choose a verse for the children to learn or review. Print each phrase of the verse (and reference) on a separate strip of construction paper. The strips and printing should be large enough for the class to read from a distance. Then tape the strips to a wall in this manner: Place the first strip high and to the left; place the second strip just under it and a little to the right; place the third strip under the second and a little further to the right. A stairway image will appear. (See page 88.)

Have the children be seated where all can see the verse stairway. Point to each stairstep and read it together. Do this a few times until the verse is familiar to the children. Then remove one stairstep from the verse and have the children repeat the entire verse. Remove another stairstep, and again have the class say the verse. If the verse is long or difficult, you could put back a phrase already removed and remove a different one. Continue in this manner until the children can say the whole verse without looking at the stairway.

If the children need to move around or stretch, have them pretend to climb a stairway (in place) as they say the verse. Or have the kids crouch down low and rise up "one step" on each phrase of the verse.

2. Build the Bricks

Supplies: Brown paper grocery bags, marker, scissors, masking tape

Preparation: Select a Bible verse that emphasizes the lesson or reviews a Sunday school memory verse. From brown paper, cut one large brick shape for each word of the verse. Clearly print the words on the bricks.

Tape each word of the verse to a wall to "build" a building. Say each word as you tape it up and have the children repeat it. When complete, read the verse together as you point to each brick. Remove one brick, and help the class say the whole verse, including the missing word. Replace that brick and remove another; again repeat the verse. Do this several more times to help the children learn the verse.

Remove all the bricks, and ask for two volunteers to work together to tape them back up in the correct order. Then have the whole class say the verse. Repeat with other children as time permits.

3. Giant Hearts

Supplies: Four or five sheets of different colored construction paper, marker

Preparation: Choose a memory verse that reinforces the lesson or reviews a verse from Sunday school. Divide the verse and reference into four or five natural segments. Cut an equal number of very large hearts from construction paper, each a different color. In large letters, print the verse and reference segments on the hearts so that when the hearts are laid out beside one another, the entire verse can be read.

Have four or five helpers stand up front holding the paper verse hearts so that the class can see them in order. Read the verse aloud, pointing to each heart as you read. Do this a few times to help nonreaders. Associating different phrases of the verse with different colors will help all the children learn it. Invite the children to join you in repeating the verse as it becomes familiar to them.

Ask one helper to turn over his paper heart, still holding it up so the color shows. Help the class say the whole verse, including the missing words. Then have that helper show the words again while a different helper turns over her paper heart. Again say the verse. Have the class repeat the verse in this manner until they can say it by just looking at the colored hearts, without needing the words.

4. Group Brainwork

Supplies: Paper, markers or colored pencils

Preparation: Choose a Bible verse to learn or review. Print the verse in large, clear letters on pieces of paper, leaving space above and beneath the words. Make a copy of it for every two or three children in your class.

Have the children work together in pairs or small groups to learn the verse. Divide the children into pairs or small groups, and give each pair or small group a prepared copy of the verse. Give out markers or colored pencils. The children help each other think of pictures that stand for words in the verse and draw them above or below the words. The pictures may be simple, as long as all the kids in that group understand what they are for. For example, they might draw a heart for "love" or an arrow pointing up for "God" or a cross for "Jesus."

Allow the children several minutes to work. Then have the groups practice saying the verse using their pictures. Remind the children to be encouraging to one another.

5. Mixed-Up Cards

Supplies: Index cards, marker

Preparation: Choose a Bible verse for the children to learn. Write each word of the Bible verse on a separate index card in large, clear printing. If the Bible verse is short and your group is large, you could make more than one set of cards.

Hand out the prepared index cards in random order to children. Have the children with cards come to the front and arrange themselves in correct order. Everyone reads the words aloud to make sure the order is correct. Then the children give their cards to other children for a turn to play.

6. Mixed-Up Words

Supplies: Scrap paper, basket or other container

Preparation: Choose a Bible verse for the children to learn. You may want to have them review a verse instead. Write each word of the verse on a separate piece of paper. Fold up the papers and put them in a basket. Make sure you have enough so that each child in your class gets a word. You might need more than one set of the verse words, depending on your class size and verse length.

Review the verse with the children a few times. Then pass around the basket with the verse words. Each child takes one word and unfolds it. Tell the children to work together to assemble the verse in the correct order. They may work on a table or the floor. When done, read it aloud in unison to check that it is right. As time permits, mix up the words and play again.

7. Paper Pass

Supplies: A crumpled newspaper

Preparation: Choose a Bible verse for the children to memorize, or choose a verse for the children to review.

Say the verse for the children, a phrase at a time, and have the class echo it after you. If you have strong readers, you could print the verse on the board and point to each word as you say it. Go over the verse several times so it becomes familiar to the children.

Have the children sit in a circle. (If your class is large, divide into two or three circles. Be sure to have a helper available to help each group.) The children pass a crumpled piece of newspaper around the circle. Whoever is touching the newspaper as it passes says the next word of the verse. Start out slowly and pick up the speed as the children learn the verse. Pass the paper the opposite direction the next time the children say the verse.

8. Popcorn

Supplies: Paper, pen

Preparation: Choose a Bible verse for the children to memorize. It may be one they've already started working on or a new one for a lesson. Write each word or phrase of the verse on individual slips of paper. Make enough sets so that every child in the class has one.

Play "Popcorn" to help the children practice the verse in a fun way. Have the children sit in a circle. Mix up the verse papers and give one to every child. At your signal, the child holding the first word or phrase of the verse pops up and reads it aloud, and then pops back down. (If more than one child is holding that part of the verse, they do it together.) The kids with the next word or phrase immediately pop up and call out their part. Then the next child or children continue with the third part. Keep playing until the whole verse has been "popped." Play several times, encouraging the children to be alert and listen for their turn so they can pop up and down rapidly like popping popcorn.

9. Put Yourself in Order

Supplies: Paper, marker, tape

Preparation: Choose a Bible verse for the children to memorize, either a new one or a review verse. Print each word of the verse on a separate sheet of paper in large letters. You will need a paper for each child.

Say the verse slowly, phrase by phrase. Repeat the verse several times until the children think they know the verse. Tape a piece of paper to the back of each child.

Give the children time to discover which word is on which back and then organize themselves in verse order. When all the children are lined up, read the verse aloud in the order displayed. Encourage them to work together to fix out-of-order words. Then say the verse together as a class.

10. Rainbow Reminders

Supplies: Construction paper in five colors, scissors, glue, pencils

Preparation: Choose a Bible verse to learn or review. From construction paper cut strips in either straight lines or curves like a rainbow, whichever works best for you. (See page 96.) Have a strip of each color for every child in your class, plus one extra straight strip (any color) for each child.

Today we'll make rainbows to help us remember our Bible memory verse. Give each child five colored strips to lay down beside one another like a rainbow. The sixth strip should be glued at one end of the rainbow to connect the five colors. The rainbow will be loose at the other end.

Print today's memory verse on the board. Have the children copy the verse onto one side of their rainbow, spacing it out so that some words are on each strip.

Lead the children in reading the verse from their rainbows. Then have the kids bend one strip back (without creasing it) so that they can't see the words on that strip. It's okay for children to choose different strips. Say the verse in unison, including the missing words. Let the children drop that strip back down and bend back a different one. Repeat the verse. Continue in this manner until the children can say the verse without looking.

Be sure the kids write their names on the glued-end strip. Set the Rainbow Reminders aside.

As I have LOVED YOU. SO YOU MUST LOVE ONE ANOTHER. John 13:34

11. Scripture Scroll

Supplies: Butcher paper, masking tape, marker
Preparation: Choose a Bible verse for the children to memorize. Hang a long length of butcher paper on a wall. Roll it up from the bottom so it looks like a scroll, and lightly tape it to hold it.

Show the children the giant "scroll" on the wall. Say the memory verse to the class. Unroll the scroll, and neatly print each word of the verse in huge letters as you say each aloud. Have the children repeat each word after you. Spread the verse out so it fills up the scroll.

Have the class read the verse with you again as you point to each word. Then roll up the scroll. Have the class say the first line; then unroll the scroll far enough for the first line to show. See if the kids got it right. Have the children say the next portion of the verse. Unroll the scroll further to check their accuracy. Continue until the whole verse has been said.

Continue rolling and unrolling the scroll as the children say the verse to give them more practice.

12. Verse Mix-up

Supplies: Paper, marker
Preparation: Choose a Bible verse for the children to review or learn. Print each word of the verse on a separate sheet of paper.

Write the verse on the board, and say it together several times. Then hand out the papers with the verse words on them. Without looking at the verse on the board, children try to arrange themselves in the correct order. Then they can repeat the verse in unison again. If your class is large, try this in two teams, seeing which team can get themselves correctly arranged first.

13. Word Cut-Outs

Supplies: Paper, marker, scissors for each group

Preparation: Write the Bible verse in large, clear printing on a piece of construction paper, leaving large spaces between the words. Make one verse paper for every three or four children. The memory verse you choose could be one the children are reviewing or a new one.

Divide the children in groups of three or four. Give each group a copy of the Bible verse and a pair of scissors. Instruct the groups to place their verse paper on the floor in the middle of their small group. Read the verse aloud together. Then have one child in each group cut out a word. The groups say the verse together again, including the word that is now missing. (The missing word will be different for each group.) Then let another child from each group cut out another word. The groups say the verse again. Continue until all words have been cut out.

When finished, let the members of each group work together to put their verse words back together in the right order.

Notes

Notes

Puzzle Games

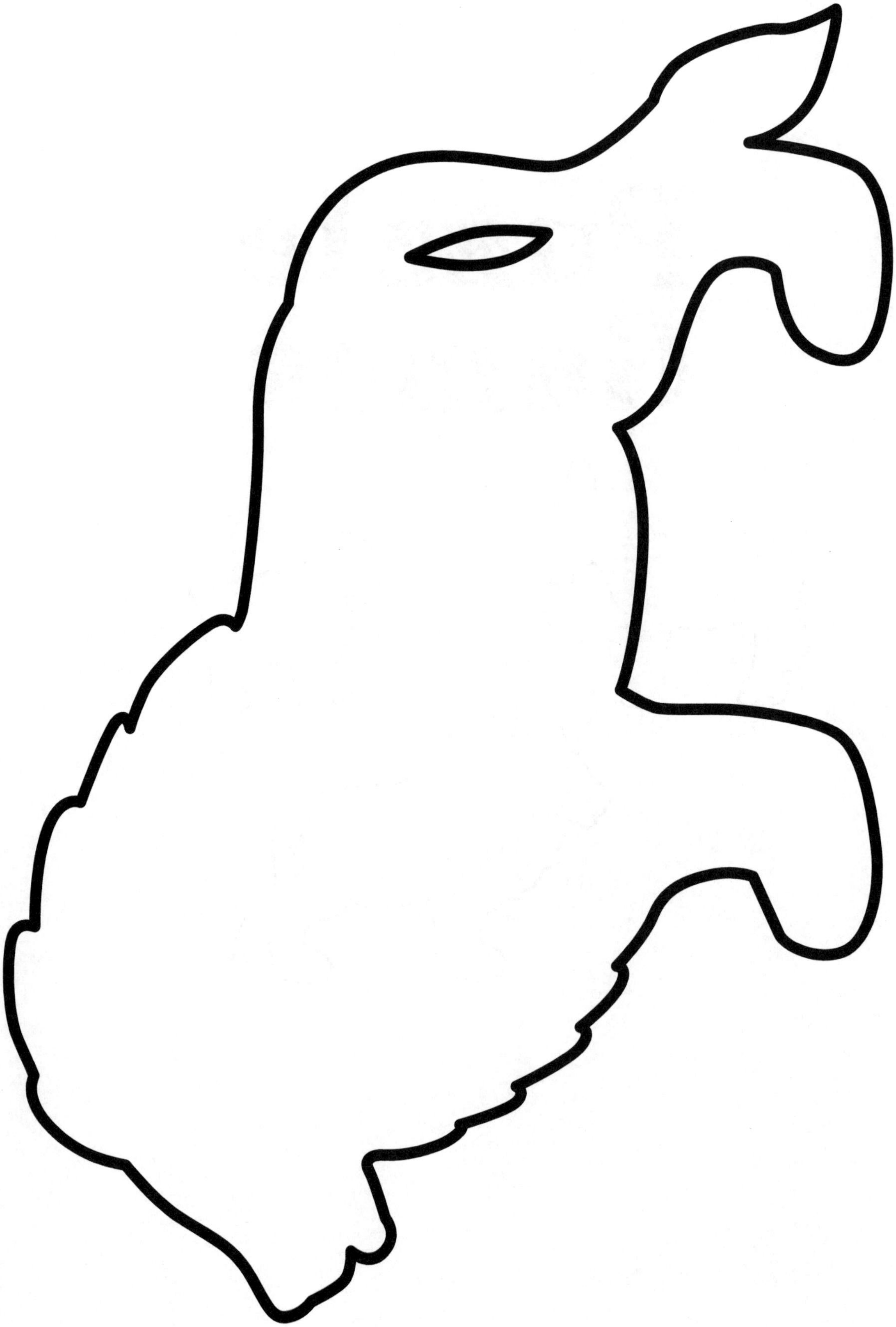

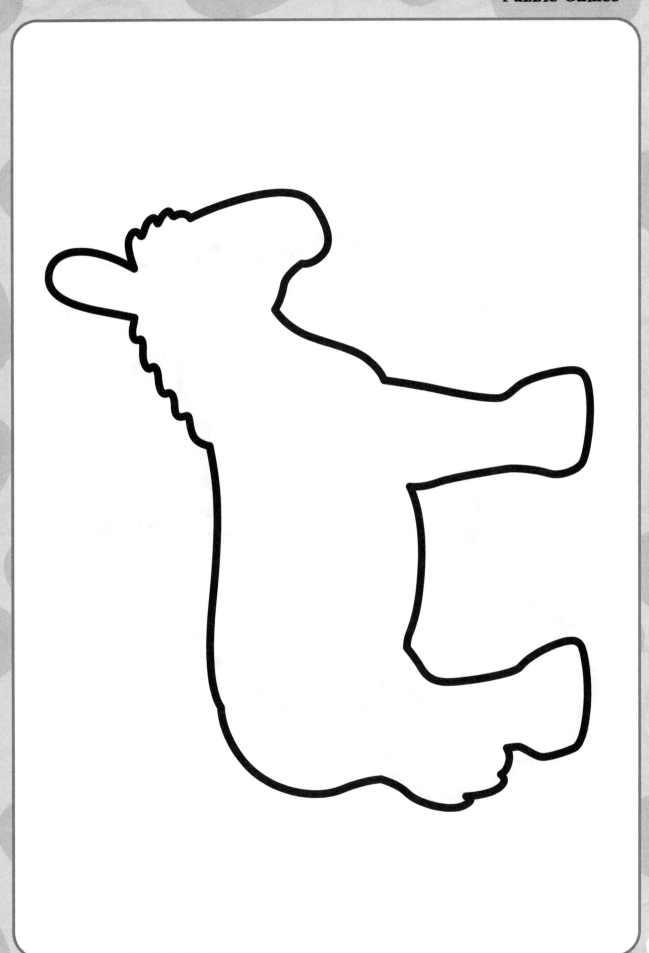

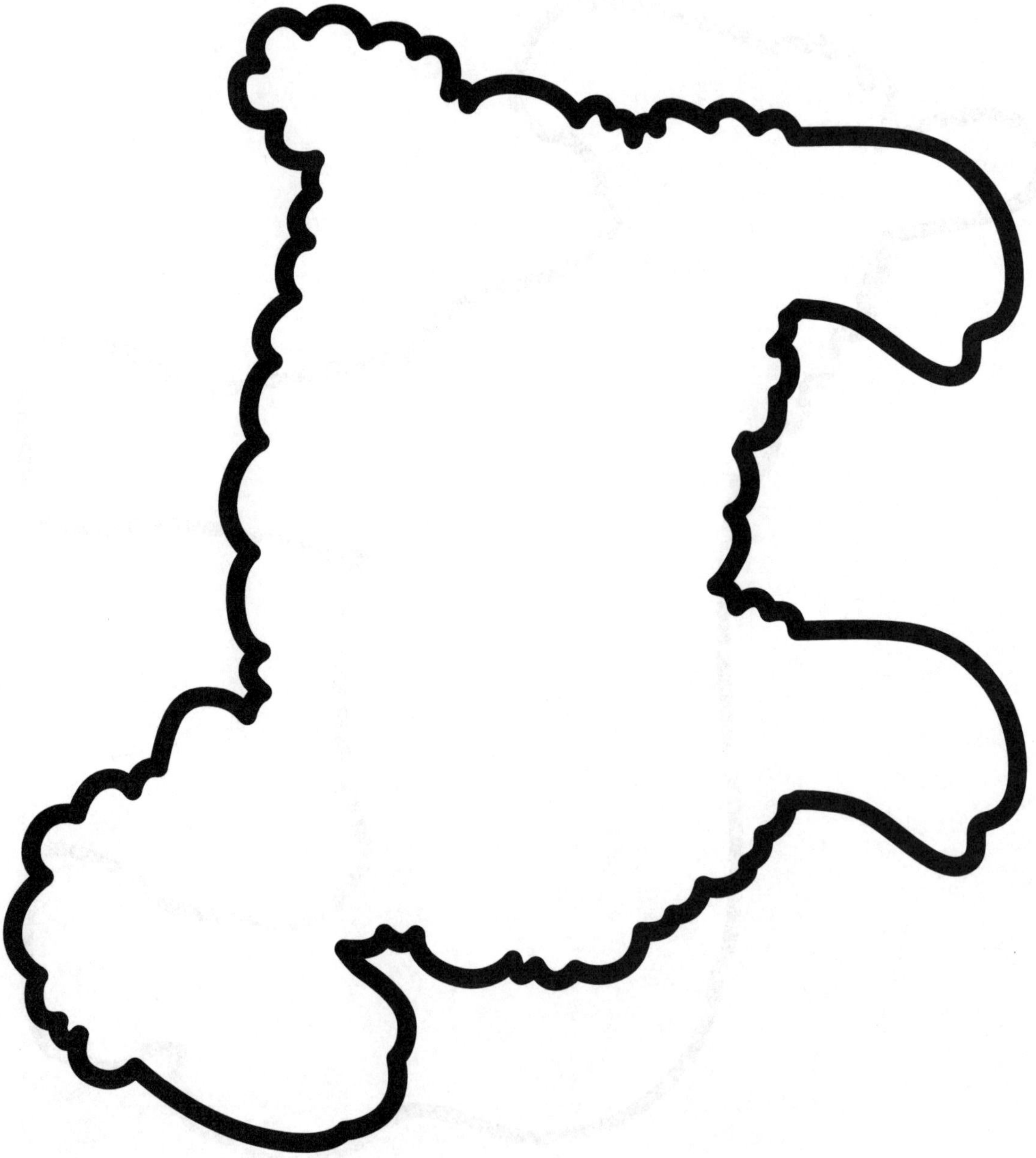

1. Animal-Verse Puzzle

Supplies: Enlarged copies of an animal outline (See pages 102–104.), stiff paper, scissors, (optional: clear, self-adhesive paper, various other animal outlines)

Preparation: Select a Bible verse that supports the day's lesson or reviews a verse the children have been working on. Enlarge the animal outline to fill an 8 1/2" x 11" page. Print the memory verse inside the lion. Make several copies on stiff paper. Cut the pictures into large jigsaw puzzle pieces. Before cutting, you may want to cover the picture with clear, self-adhesive paper to protect and strengthen it. If you have access to other animal outlines, you may want to make several different puzzles for the children to use.

Introduce the verse by saying it to the class, a few words at a time, and having the kids repeat it after you. Divide the kids into small groups, and give each group a set of puzzle pieces. Let the small groups work together to assemble their animal-verse puzzles. After a group assembles their puzzle, they say the verse together. Then they may mix up the pieces and do it again. The more times the kids do the puzzle, the better they will learn the verse.

2. Basket of Words

Supplies: Paper, pencil, basket or other container

Preparation: Choose a Bible verse that supports the lesson. Print each word of the verse on a separate slip of paper. Also draw a symbol or picture to represent as many of the words as possible. Mix up the papers and place them in the basket. If your class is large, make two sets. Print the verse on the board.

Have everyone read along as you point to each word of the verse on the board. Be sure the children understand what all the words mean.

Then pass around the basket and have each child take one of the papers with a verse word on it. If there are more papers than children, some kids will have more than one. Have the children work together to lay the papers on the floor in the correct order. When completed, have the whole class say the verse aloud.

3. Card Mix-up

Supplies: Index cards, marker

Preparation: Choose a Bible verse for the children to memorize. Neatly print each word of the verse on index cards. Also include small sketches or stickers that give clues to the words (for nonreaders). On the back, number the cards in the correct order. Make enough sets of verse cards so that every group of three children has a set. Keep the sets in order to start with.

Divide the children into groups of three, and give each group a set of verse cards. For groups with nonreaders, have a helper join them.

Instruct the groups to lay out their cards in order. Read the verse aloud together.

Tell the children to mix up their cards. Then encourage the groups to work together to put the cards back in the correct order. Groups may check their verse by looking at the numbers on the back.

When all the groups have their verse together correctly, lead the class in saying the verse together. Mix up the cards and continue to play until the children are confident of the verse.

4. Cleaning the Temple

Supplies: One sheet of newsprint paper, marker, scissors, masking tape

Preparation: Choose a Bible verse that supports the lesson or use this activity to review a verse the children memorized earlier. Lay a sheet of newsprint paper sideways, and print the words of the verse and reference in large, clear letters, filling up the whole page. Make the page into a scroll by rolling it from both sides until the rolls meet in the middle. Then carefully cut the scroll into four or five pieces. Hide the scroll pieces around the room.

This activity works well with the story of Ezra reading the scroll. Tell the children your room has gotten as messy as the temple in Old Testament times and ask them to help you find a scroll. Allow a minute for the children to find the scroll pieces. Then have the kids be seated.

Oh, no! Our scroll is in pieces! I can't read it. Unroll one scroll piece, and let the children read the words or word parts that are on it. Do the same with the other pieces. **I know that our verse goes like this.** Say the verse correctly for the children. Say it again, phrase by phrase, and have the kids repeat it after you. Say it together a few more times until the verse is familiar to the children.

Have child helpers stand along the front and hold open the scroll pieces. Let the class give directions for where the helpers should move in order for the scroll pieces to be in the correct order. When correct, have the helpers hold the scroll pieces close together, as if it were not cut apart, so the verse can be read. If you have sufficient time, let other children have a turn to hold the scroll while the rest of the children direct them to stand in the correct order. Be sure to have the children say the verse aloud as they direct the children to the correct order.

5. Paper Person

Supplies: Butcher paper, marker, scissors, masking tape

Preparation: Choose a Bible verse for the children to memorize or review. Draw or trace the outline of a person on a length of butcher paper. Cut out the outline, and then cut the outline into major body parts—two legs, two arms, a torso, and a head. Divide the verse and reference into six parts, and write each on a different body part. Place rolls of masking tape, sticky side out, on the back of each body part so it will stick to the wall when needed.

Say the verse for the children a few times. Be sure they understand what all the words mean. Then let six volunteers come up and each hold one of the body parts. Have them each read their part (help any nonreaders), and then correctly put together the body by taping it to a wall. Have the class say the verse together.

Take down the body parts, and let six more kids come up, read their verse portion, and hang up the body again. Have the whole class repeat the verse. Continue until all the kids have had a chance to assemble the paper-person Bible verse.

6. Pillowcase Puzzles

Supplies: Decorative pillowcases, poster board or cardstock paper, scissors, crayons or markers

Preparation: Choose a Bible verse to use with the activity. Cut poster board into strips about three inches wide. On each strip, print the memory verse in large, clear letters, leaving an inch or two between each word. Cut between each word in a zigzag or curved fashion to make the puzzle. You can make your cuts more difficult for older children. Place each set of puzzle pieces in a separate pillowcase. Make one Pillowcase Puzzle for each group of four children in your class.

Say the verse together with the class a few times. Then divide the children into groups of four. Give each group a pillowcase with precut verse puzzle pieces inside. Instruct the groups to take turns pulling out puzzle pieces one at a time and working together to put their puzzle together. This activity is not a race, so encourage the kids to think through the verse to figure out the order of the words, using the puzzle lines to guide them.

For younger readers, number the backs of the puzzle pieces to show the correct word order.

7. Rebus Verse

Supplies: Newsprint or butcher paper, crayons or markers, masking tape

Preparation: Choose a memory verse that highlights the lesson or reviews a verse the children have been memorizing. If possible, choose one that can be made into a rebus (substituting pictures for some of the words or phrases). On newsprint or butcher paper, print the verse in large letters, leaving a blank space in place of some visual words or phrases. Hang the verse where all can see it.

Show the children the incomplete verse sign, and let a couple of good readers read it, omitting the missing spots. Tell the children what the missing parts are, and ask the children to help you think of pictures to draw there. Agree together on each needed picture, and sketch each in the appropriate blank spot. In between drawing each picture, have the class repeat the whole verse in unison.

When the rebus is complete, call on groups of kids, based on their clothing or age, to stand and say the verse together. For example, children wearing buckle shoes, children wearing black, children who are six years old, and so on.

8. Stained-Glass Window

Supplies: White newsprint or butcher paper, black marker, watercolor paints and brush, scissors, masking tape

Preparation: Choose a Bible verse that supports the lesson. Use a marker to draw the outline of a stained-glass window. Clearly print the verse inside the window. Then draw wavy or diagonal lines to form various-sized windowpanes. Use watercolor paints to lightly paint the different panes so the words are readable. When dry, cut apart the panes and then lightly tape them to a wall showing the assembled window.

Read the verse to the children, pointing to each word. Read the verse together a few more times.

Invite a child to remove one of the panes. Say the verse again, including the missing section. Ask another child to remove another pane. Repeat the verse. Continue until all panes are gone. Repeat the verse from memory a few times.

9. Verse Puzzle

Supplies: Poster board or butcher paper, markers, scissors

Preparation: Choose a verse that supports the lesson. Print the verse and reference on poster board or butcher paper. Cut it into large puzzle pieces, so there are 2–3 words or parts of words on each piece. If you have a large class, make two or three verse puzzles in this manner.

Lead in reciting the verse several times by saying a few words and having the class repeat it after you. Be sure that all the children understand the verse.

Hand out the verse puzzle pieces and ask the children to work together to put it together. Once completed, have them recite it again. As time permits, let the kids mix up the puzzles and assemble them again.

10. Verse Sails

Supplies: Large paper, scissors, marker

Preparation: Print the verse on large paper shaped like a sail. Cut the sail vertically into long wavy strips. Make enough sails to accommodate four or five kids per group.

Use the following activity to help the children learn a Bible verse of your choice.

Divide the class into groups of four or five children each. Give each group a copy of the prepared verse sail. After reviewing the verse together, ask the groups to figure out their sail puzzle by putting the words in the right order. When finished, have each group read its verse in unison. As time permits, the groups may trade puzzles and play again.

Scripture Pictures

Bring the Bible to Life with 52 Visually-Interactive Bible Stories for Kids!

Lessons in English and Spanish!

Every lesson is easy to teach—in English or Spanish! You'll love the flexible design—the built-in easel makes it easy to use with your kids. Use it alone or as an extra resource for your Sunday school class or midweek program. All 52 age-appropriate Bible stories will inspire your kids to walk through the Old Testament and discover more about God. Each lesson comes with Bible Background to help the teacher prepare, engaging Application Questions, and a fun Review Activity.

A Journey Through the Old Testament
#103433; ISBN: 0-78144-074-2

Experiencing the Life of Christ
#103247; ISBN: 0-78144-032-7

52 pages, 4-color Bible art, 52 pages of Bible story material
17 x 11, Spiral bound
$29.99 *(Canada $44.99)*

Creative Bible Activities for Children

100's of Songs, Games and More!

Bring the Bible to life and help your kids stay interested in learning with these fun activities, songs and crafts! Over 1200 action-packed ideas at your fingertips. $16.99 *(Can. $24.99)*

Preschoolers
ISBN: 0-78143-966-3 ITEM #: 102859
8.5 x 11, 157p

School Kids
ISBN: 0-78143-965-5 ITEM #: 102858
8.5 x 11, 143p

One Rehearsal Christmas Plays
$12.99   ISBN 0-78144-120-X
ITEM #: 103618   8.5 x 11, 96p

Bible Memory Games
$16.99 *(Can. $24.99)* ISBN 0-78144-119-6
ITEM #: 103617   8.5 x 11, 143p

Spur-of-the-Moment Crafts
$12.99; ISBN 0-78144-121-8; ITEM #: 103619

Spur-of-the-Moment Games
$12.99; ISBN 0-78144-118-8; ITEM #: 103616

Life and Lessons of Jesus Series
(4-Volume Series)

Make Jesus real for kids with reproducible, easy-to-do and fun activities! Each volume is packed with dozens of projects that you won't find anywhere else!

$24.99 each *(Can. $37.99)*, 8 1/2 x 11, PB

Vol 1—Jesus' Early Years
ISBN: 0-78143-847-0
ITEM #: 101841

Vol 3—Following Jesus
ISBN: 0-78143-849-7
ITEM #: 101843

Vol 2—Jesus' Ministry
ISBN: 0-78143-848-9
ITEM #: 101842

Vol 4—The Love of Jesus
ISBN: 0-78143-850-0
ITEM #: 101844

The Word at Work Around the World

What would you do if you wanted to share God's love with children on the streets of your city? That's the dilemma David C. Cook faced in 1870's Chicago. His answer was to create literature that would capture children's hearts.

Out of those humble beginnings grew a worldwide ministry that has used literature to proclaim God's love and disciple generation after generation. Cook Communications Ministries is committed to personal discipleship—to helping people of all ages learn God's Word, embrace His salvation, walk in His ways, and minister in His name.

Faith Kidz, RiverOak, Honor, Life Journey, Victor, NextGen . . . every time you purchase a book produced by Cook Communications Ministries, you not only meet a vital personal need in your life or in the life of someone you love, but you're also a part of ministering to José in Colombia, Humberto in Chile, Gousa in India, or Lidiane in Brazil. You help make it possible for a pastor in China, a child in Peru, or a mother in West Africa to enjoy a life-changing book. And because you helped, children and adults around the world are learning God's Word and walking in His ways.

Thank you for your partnership in helping to disciple the world. May God bless you with the power of His Word in your life.

For more information about our international ministries, visit www.ccmi.org.